TABLE OF CONTENT

Chapter 1: The Early Years
- Childhood and passion for racing
- Karting success and rise through the ranks ... 4

Chapter 2: Formula 1 Debut ... 6
- Entry into Formula 1 with Toleman ... 6
- Move to Lotus and first race wins ... 7

Chapter 3: The McLaren Era ... 10
- Partnership with McLaren and dominance ... 10
- Three World Championships and countless victories ... 12

Chapter 4: Williams Years and the Return ... 15
- Transfer to Williams and pursuit of a fourth title ... 15
- Departure from Williams and brief retirement ... 16

Chapter 5: Legacy and Impact ... 19
- Tragic accident at Imola ... 19
- Impact on the racing world and beyond ... 21
- Posthumous honors and tributes ... 22

Chapter 6: Beyond the Track ... 25
- Senna's activism and humanitarian efforts ... 25
- Advocacy for safety improvements in motorsport ... 27

Chapter 7: Technical Prowess 30

    Senna's innovative driving style and exceptional car control 30

    Contributions to advancements in Formula 1 technology 32

Chapter 8: Psychological Warfare 34

    Senna's mental fortitude and competitive edge 34

    Use of on-track mind games and aggression 35

Chapter 9: Controversies and Rivalries 38

    Notable incidents and confrontations 38

    Rivalry with Alain Prost 40

Chapter 10: The Human Side 43

    Senna's personality, values, and personal relationships 43

    Struggles and triumphs off the track 45

Chapter 11: The Legend Lives On 48

    Senna's enduring popularity and cultural impact 48

    Museums, memorials, and ongoing tributes 50

Chapter 12: Lessons from Senna 53

    Analysis of his driving techniques, strategies, and mindset 53

    Inspiring lessons for racers, athletes, and beyond 55

Chapter 13: A Sporting Icon 57

    Senna's place among the greatest athletes of all time 57

Recognition for his achievements and character 59

Chapter 14: The Spirit of Senna 62

The enduring legacy of his spirit and determination 62

Influence on generations of racers and fans 64

Chapter 15: The Unforgettable 67

A fitting tribute to Ayrton Senna's extraordinary life and career 67

A testament to his lasting impact on the world of motorsport 69

Chapter 1: The Early Years

Childhood and passion for racing

Ayrton Senna da Silva, a name synonymous with racing prowess and unparalleled passion, was born on March 21, 1960, in São Paulo, Brazil. The seeds of his extraordinary journey were sown in the fertile ground of his childhood, nurtured by a deep-seated love for speed and a profound connection to the world of motorsports. Even in his early years, the young Senna exhibited an innate talent for speed and a fascination with machines. From a tender age, his world revolved around the roar of engines and the adrenaline rush of defying gravity. His father, Milton da Silva, was a successful businessman who instilled in his son a strong work ethic and a relentless pursuit of excellence. Milton, himself a passionate racing enthusiast, introduced Ayrton to the exhilarating world of motorsports. At the age of four, Senna's insatiable curiosity was sparked by his first encounter with a go-kart, a miniature racing vehicle that would forever alter the course of his life. It was a fateful meeting that ignited a lifelong passion and set him on a trajectory destined for greatness.

The simple act of driving a go-kart ignited an uncontrollable fire within young Ayrton. He was captivated by the sense of freedom, the thrill of competition, and the challenge of mastering the intricacies of speed and control. His parents, recognizing the intensity of his passion, nurtured his burgeoning talent by providing him with the resources and opportunities to pursue his racing dreams. In the early 1970s, a small go-kart track in Interlagos, São Paulo, became his playground, a sanctuary where he could hone his skills and cultivate his natural abilities. There, under the watchful eyes of his father and mentors, he began to sculpt his driving style, developing a unique blend of aggression, precision, and an almost supernatural understanding of the machine. .

Driven by a relentless hunger for success, Senna's talent quickly blossomed, leaving his peers in his wake. His mastery of the go-kart, a seemingly simple machine, revealed a raw talent that transcended the limitations of age and experience. He possessed a natural aptitude for reading the track, anticipating the movements of his opponents, and extracting the maximum performance from the tiny racing machine. His competitive spirit burned brightly, fueled by an unwavering determination to win and an indomitable spirit that refused to accept defeat.

However, Senna's rise was not without its challenges. As his talent blossomed, so did the realization that his dreams extended beyond the confines of a local go-kart track. To further his ambitions, he needed to embrace a more challenging environment, one that would push him to the limits of his abilities. In 1977, at the age of seventeen, Senna embarked on a bold decision, one that would forever shape his destiny: he moved to England. The move marked a turning point in his career, exposing him to a new level of competition and the demanding standards of European motorsport.

England was a crucible, a testing ground where Senna's skills were forged in the fires of fierce competition and relentless pursuit of excellence. He immersed himself in the British racing scene, competing against seasoned drivers in a higher echelon of motorsport. This period marked a significant turning point in his development, pushing him beyond his comfort zone and forcing him to adapt to unfamiliar environments and challenges. .

However, Senna's journey to the pinnacle of motorsport was not a smooth one. His passion for racing, his unwavering determination, and his relentless pursuit of excellence were often overshadowed by the financial constraints that plagued his early career. In the fiercely competitive world of motorsport, where financial backing was often the deciding factor, Senna's talent was hampered by his limited resources. He tirelessly sought sponsors and support, his determination fueled by an unshakeable belief in his own abilities. .

The early years of Senna's career were marked by his relentless pursuit of excellence, his unwavering belief in his own abilities, and his unwavering desire to prove himself on the world stage. He persevered through countless challenges, his passion for racing serving as his guiding light. The sacrifices he made, the risks he took, and the unwavering belief he held in his own abilities were testament to his unwavering dedication to his craft. .

In the years that followed, Senna's relentless pursuit of excellence led him through a series of triumphs and tribulations, shaping him into the legendary driver he would become. His driving style, characterized by precision, aggression, and an almost supernatural understanding of the machine, was honed through years of dedicated training and countless hours spent on the track. He meticulously studied every aspect of racing, from the intricacies of car setup to the nuances of track conditions, constantly seeking to refine his craft and push the limits of his abilities.

His passion for racing transcended the mere pursuit of victory; it was a deep-seated love for the sport, a profound connection to the machine, and a relentless pursuit of perfection. He believed that every corner, every lap, every race presented an opportunity to push the boundaries of human potential, to redefine the very definition of speed and control. His driving style reflected this philosophy, characterized by a fearless attack, a willingness to take calculated risks, and an uncanny ability to extract the maximum performance from his car.

Senna's journey to the pinnacle of motorsport was a testament to his unwavering determination, his indomitable spirit, and his unyielding passion. He was a force of nature, a driving force that defied the odds and shattered expectations. His legacy transcends the realm of motorsports, inspiring generations with his unwavering belief in the pursuit of excellence, his relentless drive to achieve the impossible, and his profound respect for the sport he loved. .

Karting success and rise through the ranks

Ayrton Senna da Silva, born on March 21, 1960, in São Paulo, Brazil, was destined for greatness. The son of Milton da Silva, a successful entrepreneur, and Neyde Senna, a woman of unwavering support, Ayrton's life was a tapestry woven with threads of passion, dedication, and an indomitable spirit. His early childhood was marked by a profound fascination with speed and a love for all things mechanical. While his peers indulged in typical childhood pastimes, Ayrton's imagination was captured by the roar of engines and the thrill of the race. This innate fascination, a seed planted in his formative years, would blossom into an extraordinary journey that would rewrite the annals of motorsport history.

The genesis of Ayrton Senna's illustrious career lay not on the asphalt of Formula One circuits, but on the modest tracks of the karting world. At the tender age of four, a miniature go-kart, a Christmas gift from his father, became his first foray into the world of competitive racing. This seemingly innocuous toy, with its tiny engine and simple design, ignited a spark within him. As he navigated the makeshift tracks of his family's estate, a natural talent began to surface. The precision of his driving, the strategic approach to every corner, and the unwavering determination he displayed, were all telltale signs of a future champion in the making. .

Driven by an insatiable passion, young Ayrton yearned for more challenging tracks and competitive environments. He began participating in local karting competitions, racing against seasoned veterans despite his age. His initial forays into this competitive world were marked by a mix of triumphs and setbacks. The victories, however, were more than mere trophies. They fueled his ambition, pushing him to refine his skills and relentlessly pursue perfection. .

His father, recognizing the potential within his son, provided unwavering support. The elder Senna, a man who understood the demands of competitive sports, invested in better equipment and encouraged Ayrton's pursuit of excellence. He even went so far as to create a makeshift workshop, a haven of tools and ingenuity, where they would meticulously work on the karts, transforming them into extensions of their combined vision.

The early years were a crucible of experience, shaping Ayrton into a formidable competitor. He honed his skills on the tight, twisting tracks, learning the nuances of karting, the art of overtaking, and the crucial importance of race strategy. His innate talent, coupled with the unwavering dedication he displayed, earned him recognition within the local karting community. His victories were not mere chance occurrences; they were a testament to his meticulous preparation, his laser-sharp focus, and a relentless pursuit of perfection that set him apart from his peers. .

While the karting tracks were a proving ground for his talent, it was the camaraderie and the fierce rivalry he encountered that truly shaped him. These experiences, while sometimes brutal in their competitive nature, instilled in him a respect for his opponents and an unwavering belief in his own capabilities. He learned the value of sportsmanship, the importance of pushing one's limits, and the realization that the path to victory is rarely paved with ease. .

The karting years were more than just a prelude to a glorious future. They were the foundational pillars on which Ayrton Senna would build his legacy. The grit, the determination, the strategic brilliance, and the unwavering pursuit of excellence he honed during these formative years would become defining characteristics of his driving style and his enduring legacy as a racing icon.

Chapter 2: Formula 1 Debut

Entry into Formula 1 with Toleman

The year was 1984, and Ayrton Senna, a young driver with an insatiable thirst for speed and a burgeoning reputation, stood at the precipice of his Formula 1 dreams. After dominating the British Formula 3 Championship, Senna's talent had caught the eye of several teams, but it was the Toleman team, a small, independent outfit with a daring spirit, that offered him his ticket to the grand prix stage.

The Toleman TG184, designed by Rory Byrne, was a car that promised potential but struggled with reliability. It was a machine that required a driver with exceptional skill and daring to unlock its true performance. Senna, with his lightning-fast reflexes and audacious driving style, proved to be the perfect match.

His debut at the Brazilian Grand Prix, his home race, was a baptism by fire. Although the car lacked the pace of the established teams, Senna's sheer talent shone through. He qualified an impressive 17th, surpassing the expectations of many who had written him off as a rookie. He battled through the early laps, gaining positions with breathtaking precision and a boldness that surprised seasoned veterans. His race ended prematurely due to a mechanical failure, but the seeds of his legend had been sown.

Senna's next race, the San Marino Grand Prix, marked a turning point in his career. The Toleman, plagued by reliability issues, had qualified a lowly 16th. But Senna, fueled by an unyielding determination and a fierce competitive spirit, weaved through the field with breathtaking speed and precision. He carved his way past established drivers with calculated aggression, showcasing his remarkable talent for overtaking and racecraft. .

Rain began to fall as the race progressed, transforming the track into a treacherous river of asphalt. The drivers, with the exception of the leading trio, were advised by their teams to slow down due to the dangerous conditions. Yet, Senna, unfazed by the treacherous conditions and undeterred by the advice of his team, pushed the limits of both his car and his own abilities. He drove with breathtaking audacity, his car dancing precariously on the edge of control. .

As the race reached its climax, Senna was closing in on the leaders, having already passed several drivers with audacious maneuvers. He was poised to achieve a stunning result, potentially even a podium finish, when the race was prematurely stopped due to a fatal accident that claimed the life of Ferrari driver, Jochen Mass. Senna's drive, however, had sent shockwaves through the paddock. The world had glimpsed the raw, untamed brilliance that lay within the young Brazilian.

His performance at San Marino, despite the tragic circumstances, cemented his reputation as a force to be reckoned with. His driving style, characterized by an almost reckless pursuit of victory, earned him both admiration and criticism. While some saw his boldness as recklessness, others recognized it as a testament to his unwavering focus and his insatiable desire to win. Senna's time with Toleman, though brief, was a crucible that forged his legend. It was a period of immense learning and growth, where he honed his skills, tested his limits, and began to establish himself as a future champion. The seeds sown in those early races would blossom into a career that would redefine Formula 1 and cement his place as one of the greatest drivers of all time.

Move to Lotus and first race wins

The 1984 season marked a pivotal juncture in Senna's burgeoning career. Having conquered Formula 3 in 1983, he transitioned to the world of Formula 1, joining the legendary Team Lotus. This move, while seemingly a natural progression, brought with it a whirlwind of new challenges. .

The Lotus 95T, designed by the brilliant Gerard Ducarouge, was a car of incredible potential, yet its technical complexities presented a steep learning curve for the young Brazilian. Senna, however, was not one to be deterred. His unwavering dedication to meticulous preparation and tireless pursuit of perfection quickly endeared him to the team. He spent countless hours studying the car's intricate mechanics, tirelessly analyzing data and strategizing with his engineers. This meticulous approach, coupled with his raw talent, was evident in the very first race of the season at Brazil. .

While he failed to secure a podium finish in his home race, Senna's performance was nothing short of a revelation. His blistering pace and fearless driving style left the paddock buzzing with anticipation. The young driver, with his signature aggressive driving and audacious overtaking maneuvers, immediately captured the attention of the F1 world. .

The following races further solidified Senna's reputation as a force to be reckoned with. His tenacity and ability to extract the maximum from the Lotus 95T earned him valuable points, including a coveted second-place finish at the Monaco Grand Prix. The principality, renowned for its challenging circuit and unforgiving walls, became a testament to Senna's skill and courage.

The momentum continued through the season, with Senna securing a remarkable pole position at the Belgian Grand Prix. Although he ultimately finished third, his performance showcased his innate talent and ability to adapt to any situation. His determination to succeed was palpable, evident in the way he relentlessly pushed the limits of both himself and the car.

The 1984 season, while ultimately failing to deliver a championship title, proved to be a crucial steppingstone in Senna's journey to becoming a legend. His performances showcased his raw talent, his unwavering dedication, and his extraordinary ability to push boundaries. This season was not just about proving his worth; it was about laying the groundwork for a future filled with triumphs and accolades. .

Senna's first F1 victory came in 1985, a season that saw him emerge as a true contender. His victory at the Portuguese Grand Prix was a testament to his relentless spirit and unwavering focus. He outpaced his competitors with his remarkable driving skills and a shrewd race strategy. .

This victory, his first in Formula 1, was a moment etched in history. It cemented his status as a formidable driver, a force to be reckoned with. The world of Formula 1 had witnessed the birth of a legend. .

The subsequent victory at the Belgian Grand Prix further solidified Senna's dominance. His ability to control the race from the front, showcasing unparalleled precision and strategic prowess, left spectators spellbound. He once again demonstrated his remarkable talent and the unwavering pursuit of victory that would become his hallmark. .

His triumph at the Monaco Grand Prix in 1987 marked another milestone in his burgeoning career. The victory, achieved in a rain-soaked race, became synonymous with his mastery of wet conditions. He had earned the title of "Rain Master," a label that further cemented his reputation as a fearless and formidable driver. .

These early victories, while individually significant, were also crucial in shaping Senna's legacy. They were a testament to his relentless pursuit of perfection, his meticulous approach to racing, and his unwavering belief in his abilities. He didn't simply win races; he dominated them with a ferocity and skill that left the motorsport world captivated. .

The first victories, etched into the annals of Formula 1, were merely the beginning. Senna's relentless pursuit of excellence, coupled with his unwavering passion, would propel him to greater heights, leaving behind an unforgettable legacy. His name, synonymous with speed, skill, and unwavering determination, would forever be etched into the heart of the sport.

Chapter 3: The McLaren Era

Partnership with McLaren and dominance

Ayrton Senna's partnership with McLaren, commencing in 1988, marked a turning point in Formula One history. It wasn't just a collaboration between driver and team; it was a marriage of raw talent and technological brilliance, a fusion of human ambition and engineering prowess. The result was a period of dominance that redefined the sport, etching Senna's name in racing folklore.

McLaren, under the visionary leadership of Ron Dennis, had meticulously cultivated a team driven by innovation and an obsessive pursuit of perfection. This philosophy aligned perfectly with Senna's own relentless drive and commitment to excellence. From the moment he stepped into the cockpit of the iconic MP4/4, it was clear that something special was brewing. The car, powered by a Honda engine, was a masterpiece of engineering, boasting an unprecedented level of aerodynamic efficiency and raw power. Coupled with Senna's exceptional talent, it proved to be an unstoppable force on the track.

The 1988 season was a testament to their potent synergy. Senna, in his first year with McLaren, secured a dominant victory at the Brazilian Grand Prix, his home race, setting the tone for the season. He went on to win 16 out of 16 races, securing the World Championship title with an astonishing 14 wins. It was a feat that defied precedent, cementing Senna's status as a legend.

The following year, 1989, presented a different challenge. The team faced stiff competition from Ferrari, and Senna's teammate, Alain Prost, proved to be a formidable opponent. The season was marked by intense rivalry and tactical maneuvers, culminating in the infamous incident at the Japanese Grand Prix. The clash between the two titans of the sport, both vying for the championship, was a pivotal moment that defined their relationship and the future of Formula One.

Despite the turmoil, Senna continued to exhibit his extraordinary talent. He secured another World Championship title in 1990, showcasing his ability to rise above adversity. He continued to push the boundaries of performance, leaving an indelible mark on the sport. His driving style, characterized by its finesse and precision, revolutionized the way Formula One was approached. He was a master of the car, seamlessly adapting to its nuances and pushing its limits.

The McLaren-Senna partnership transcended mere professional collaboration. It was a harmonious fusion of two forces, each contributing to a phenomenal performance. Senna's talent, honed by years of relentless dedication, found an ideal canvas in McLaren's innovative and technologically advanced machinery. Together, they redefined the very essence of Formula One racing, setting a new standard for speed and precision.

The success of the partnership wasn't just about winning races; it was about pushing boundaries, redefining limits, and pushing the sport forward. Senna's commitment to excellence, coupled with McLaren's unwavering pursuit of innovation, sparked a revolution in the world of motorsports. It was a period marked by brilliance and dominance, etched forever in the annals of racing history.

Beyond the tangible victories and championships, the McLaren-Senna partnership resonated on a deeper level. It was a symbol of human ambition, an embodiment of the relentless pursuit of perfection. It inspired countless aspiring racers and captivated fans worldwide, leaving a legacy that continues to inspire and amaze.

As the partnership reached its zenith, a sense of inevitability seemed to pervade the sport. The question wasn't if Senna would win, but how he would do it. The dominance was so profound, the victories so emphatic, that it was as if Senna had defied the very fabric of the sport. He was a force of nature, a phenomenon that transcended mere sporting achievements.

Senna's impact on McLaren was profound. He not only helped the team achieve unparalleled success but also shaped its identity. His driving style, his unwavering commitment to excellence, his uncompromising spirit, all left their imprint on the team's philosophy. McLaren, under Senna's influence, became synonymous with speed, innovation, and the relentless pursuit of excellence.

The McLaren-Senna partnership was a brief but brilliant chapter in Formula One history. It was a symphony of speed and skill, a testament to the power of human ambition and technological brilliance. Their legacy lives on, a testament to the extraordinary bond between driver and car, a reminder of the enduring allure of speed and the profound impact of one man's determination to conquer.

Three World Championships and countless victories

Ayrton Senna's association with McLaren, beginning in 1988, marked the zenith of his career. It was an era defined by technological prowess, fierce rivalry, and Senna's relentless pursuit of perfection. It was within this crucible that Senna's talent blossomed, yielding three World Championships and a cascade of victories that cemented his legendary status.

The marriage of Senna with McLaren was a match made in motorsport heaven. The team, under the leadership of Ron Dennis, had become synonymous with innovation and performance. The Honda engine, coupled with the aerodynamically advanced MP4/4, provided Senna with a formidable weapon. This potent package, amplified by Senna's prodigious talent, would dominate Formula One in 1988, rewriting the sport's history in the process.

The 1988 season unfolded like a relentless march towards triumph. Senna, in the MP4/4, was simply unbeatable. His prowess behind the wheel, combined with the car's blistering speed, produced a string of victories that left rivals bewildered and demoralized. It was a dominance so comprehensive that it became almost surreal. Senna's performance in the 1988 Monaco Grand Prix, a race he dominated with an audacious, unforgettable display of skill and nerve, became the benchmark against which all future Monaco performances would be measured. .

The following season, 1989, saw a resurgence in competition, particularly from Alain Prost, Senna's teammate. The rivalry between these two titans, fueled by their contrasting driving styles and personalities, intensified the drama of the championship battle. Senna, despite claiming more victories than Prost, faced a contentious end to the season, culminating in a controversial incident at the Japanese Grand Prix. The championship slipped from his grasp, leaving a bitter taste of disappointment.

However, the 1990 season saw Senna reclaim his throne. He dominated the championship race, exhibiting a level of consistency and determination that was almost superhuman. His driving style, honed to razor-sharp precision, enabled him to extract the maximum from the MP4/5, the car he described as "an extension of myself. " He skillfully navigated the complex political landscape within the team, emerging as the undisputed leader, securing his second World Championship title.

1991 saw the emergence of a formidable rival in Nigel Mansell, who piloted a dominant Ferrari. The battle between these two titans, two of the greatest drivers of their generation, captivated the world. Senna, despite facing a formidable challenge, fought with an unwavering tenacity, never relinquishing his belief in his ability to triumph. He eventually clinched his third World Championship, solidifying his position as one of the sport's all-time greats.

The McLaren era was a defining chapter in Senna's extraordinary career. He elevated the team's performance to unprecedented heights, achieving dominance on a scale rarely witnessed in the history of Formula One. It was a period characterized by innovation, intensity, and the relentless pursuit of excellence. The victories, the accolades, the championship titles - these were all a testament to Senna's indomitable spirit and his relentless pursuit of perfection. His legacy, forged during this golden period, remains a powerful testament to his enduring greatness.

Beyond the statistics and the victories, the McLaren era encapsulated the essence of Senna's genius. His fearless approach, his meticulous attention to detail, his unwavering dedication to pushing the boundaries of what was possible - these were the qualities that defined him. He was a driver who transcended the boundaries of sport, becoming a cultural icon, a symbol of the human potential for greatness. The echoes of his triumphs, the spectacle of his daring maneuvers, the passion and brilliance he brought to the track - these are the elements that continue to inspire, and will forever remain a part of the fabric of Formula One.

Chapter 4: Williams Years and the Return

Transfer to Williams and pursuit of a fourth title

After a tumultuous period with McLaren, Ayrton Senna, the reigning World Champion, found himself at a crossroads. The acrimonious departure from the team he had helped propel to dominance was a painful experience, leaving him disillusioned with the political machinations of Formula 1. But his thirst for victory remained undimmed. The allure of a fourth World Championship, of etching his name further into the annals of racing history, was too potent to resist. .

The 1994 season presented a fresh start, a chance to reclaim the mantle of dominance. Senna's destination was the Williams team, a team synonymous with innovation and success. The pairing seemed like a match made in heaven: the most talented driver of his generation, paired with the most dominant car on the grid. The Williams FW16, designed by Adrian Newey, was a masterpiece of engineering. The car was a technological marvel, boasting active suspension and a powerful Renault engine, making it the undisputed frontrunner. .

However, the return to the top was not without its challenges. Senna, accustomed to the intricacies of the Honda engine, had to adapt to the different characteristics of the Renault power unit. The new car's active suspension system, while groundbreaking, also proved challenging to master. The car's unpredictable nature, especially in wet conditions, demanded a different approach to driving. .

The opening races of the season saw a cautious Senna, still grappling with the new car. However, the inherent brilliance of the three-time World

Champion gradually emerged. The first signs of the familiar dominance came in the San Marino Grand Prix. Though the race was marred by tragedy, with the death of his rival Roland Ratzenberger in qualifying and the fatal accident of Senna himself during the race, his performance showcased his exceptional skill and determination. .

Despite the brevity of his Williams tenure, Senna's impact on the team was profound. His driving prowess and relentless pursuit of perfection pushed the team to new heights. The Williams FW16, a car that would go on to win the 1994 championship in the hands of Damon Hill, carried the legacy of Senna's brilliance. His influence transcended his short time with the team, leaving an enduring mark on the team's ethos and the world of Formula 1. .

The tragic circumstances surrounding Senna's passing, the final race of the 1994 season in Imola, forever etched his name in the hearts and minds of racing fans. The world mourned the loss of a legend, a driver who transcended mere competition and became a symbol of human excellence. His legacy, woven into the fabric of Formula 1, continues to inspire generations of drivers and fans. His relentless pursuit of victory, his unwavering passion, and his profound impact on the sport are undeniable, ensuring that Ayrton Senna's name will forever be synonymous with greatness in the world of motorsport.

Departure from Williams and brief retirement

The end of Senna's time at Williams was marked by a shift in dynamics, a collision of personalities, and a final act of defiance. It was a story of ambition, frustration, and ultimately, a bitter parting. After his dominant 1993 season, the relationship between Senna and Frank Williams had reached a point of divergence. Senna, fueled by an insatiable drive for success, had grown increasingly frustrated with the team's direction. He yearned for a more active role in the development of the car, believing that his insights and feedback were being ignored. Williams, on the other hand, remained steadfast in his management style, prioritizing the team's collective vision over the desires of any individual driver.

The 1994 season saw Senna, in his final year with Williams, face a stark reality. The FW16, a car that promised unprecedented performance, was plagued with inherent design flaws. The car was heavy, unstable, and prone to sudden, unpredictable handling changes. For Senna, who had always prided himself on his ability to push cars to their absolute limits, the FW16 was a frustrating challenge. His driving style, characterized by its precision and aggression, was ill-suited to the car's unpredictable nature. The car's flaws were further exacerbated by a lack of reliable data from the team's telemetry, a constant source of friction between Senna and Williams. He believed that the team was failing to provide him with the necessary information to understand the car's behavior and optimize its performance. This lack of communication became a festering wound, widening the already existing rift between the driver and the team.

The 1994 season was a series of near misses, with Senna constantly pushing the limits of the FW16. In the early races, he battled with the car's unpredictability, narrowly avoiding crashes and struggling to maintain his usual dominance. He fought hard, but the car's inherent limitations proved a constant hurdle. The frustration grew, and Senna's relationship with Williams reached its breaking point. Rumors swirled about Senna's potential move to another team, specifically Benetton, fueling further speculation and tension within the Williams camp.

The Imola Grand Prix, a race that would forever be etched in the annals of Formula One history, became the stage for the final act of Senna's time at Williams. It was a race marked by tragedy, controversy, and a sense of unresolved tension. The qualifying session saw Senna, fueled by a mix of frustration and determination, push the FW16 to its limits, setting a record-breaking pole position time. He was on top, but the seeds of doubt remained. The race itself was a series of near misses, a testament to the car's unpredictable nature. Senna battled the car's handling, pushing it to its limits, but the car's inherent flaws remained. The fateful accident in the seventh lap, a result of a combination of factors, including the car's unpredictable handling and an unknown mechanical failure, ended Senna's life and left the world in shock.

Senna's departure from Williams was a complex and multifaceted event, shaped by a confluence of ambition, frustration, and a clash of personalities. His death, a tragic end to a brilliant career, also marked the end of an era. The legacy of Ayrton Senna, a driver who redefined the limits of human potential and embodied the spirit of fearless pursuit, continues to resonate across the world of motorsports and beyond. .

The aftermath of the Imola Grand Prix saw a wave of emotions sweep through the racing community. Grief and disbelief filled the paddock, and the loss of Senna cast a dark shadow over the season. His death had not only taken a legend but also exposed the fragility of life and the inherent risks involved in racing at its highest level. For Williams, the tragedy was a personal blow, a profound loss of a driver who had brought the team to unparalleled success. The incident also led to a reassessment of safety protocols in Formula One, as the sport grappled with the consequences of its inherent dangers.

Senna's departure from Williams marked the end of an era, a chapter in the history of Formula One that would forever be etched in the minds of fans and drivers alike. His legend continued to grow, fueled by his undeniable talent, his fierce competitive spirit, and his unwavering pursuit of excellence. The story of Senna's time at Williams, a chapter marked by triumph and tragedy, serves as a powerful reminder of the complex dynamics at play within the world of motorsport. It is a story that transcends the boundaries of sport, offering insights into the human condition, the relentless pursuit of excellence, and the fragility of life itself.

.

.

Chapter 5: Legacy and Impact

Tragic accident at Imola

The sun beat down on the Autodromo Enzo e Dino Ferrari, the air heavy with anticipation and the intoxicating scent of racing fuel. The roar of engines reverberated across the tarmac, a symphony of speed and power. It was May 1, 1994, the San Marino Grand Prix, and the racing world was poised to witness the brilliance of Ayrton Senna, the reigning champion, the maestro of the track. But destiny had a different script in mind.

The race began under a shroud of tragedy. Just two days earlier, during qualifying, Roland Ratzenberger, a young Austrian driver, had suffered a fatal crash. The somber mood hung heavy in the air, a chilling reminder of the inherent risk that defined this exhilarating sport.

Senna, ever the perfectionist, had qualified on pole position. He led the race with his trademark precision and finesse, pulling away from the pack like a predator stalking its prey. But on the seventh lap, a collision between Jyrki Järvilehto and Rubens Barrichello, both Brazilian drivers, prompted a safety car intervention. The deployment of the safety car, a measure intended to mitigate risk, would become the tragic catalyst for a fatal turn of events. .

As the safety car led the pack, Senna, unable to comprehend the reason for its deployment, radioed his team for an explanation. His voice, usually calm and collected, held an edge of frustration. The race resumed on lap seven, the tension palpable as drivers prepared for the final sprint. .

Then, the unthinkable happened. As Senna approached the Tamburello corner, his car suddenly veered off the track, impacting a concrete wall with devastating force. The impact was brutal, the car disintegrating upon collision. A wave of shock and disbelief washed over the circuit..

Doctors rushed to his aid, but it was too late. Senna's life was tragically extinguished on the track, his legend frozen in time. The world mourned the loss of a sporting icon, a champion whose skills and charisma had captivated audiences across the globe.

The tragic accident at Imola, a horrifying culmination of mishaps, exposed the inherent risks and the fragility of life in the world of Formula One racing. It also brought into sharp focus the complex relationship between speed, technology, and human fallibility.

The impact of Senna's death reverberated beyond the world of motorsport. His passing sparked a global outpouring of grief and tributes, a testament to his extraordinary talent and the magnetic persona that transcended the boundaries of sport..

The investigation into the accident revealed a combination of factors, including a design flaw in the Williams FW16 car, Senna's own decision to push the limits of his car while under the safety car, and potential driver error. The findings of the investigation resulted in significant changes in safety regulations in Formula One, a testament to the enduring legacy of Senna's sacrifice.

The Imola tragedy served as a stark reminder of the inherent risks associated with motorsports. But it also highlighted the importance of safety regulations and the need for constant vigilance in mitigating risk..

In the aftermath of his death, Senna's legacy transcended the realm of sport. He became a symbol of courage, determination, and the pursuit of excellence. His driving prowess and the grace with which he handled his car became a benchmark for aspiring racers. But it was his humanity, his humility, and his unwavering commitment to his passion that truly resonated with millions worldwide.

Today, over two decades later, Ayrton Senna's name remains synonymous with speed, skill, and the unwavering pursuit of perfection. His legacy, etched forever in the annals of motorsport, stands as a testament to the indomitable spirit of a champion who tragically lost his life but whose impact continues to inspire generations.

Impact on the racing world and beyond

The name Ayrton Senna evokes a visceral response in the world of motorsports. Beyond the accolades and the statistics, Senna's impact resonates deeply, transcending the realm of racing and leaving an indelible mark on society at large. His legacy, built on a potent cocktail of skill, determination, and an unyielding passion for the sport, continues to inspire and influence generations, even years after his tragic passing.

Senna's impact on racing is multifaceted. His driving style, characterized by aggressive overtakes, precise control, and a fearless pursuit of the limit, revolutionized the sport. His mastery of the racetrack, particularly in the rain, earned him legendary status, a testament to his extraordinary talent and unyielding focus. He was, without doubt, one of the greatest drivers of all time, a fact acknowledged by his three Formula One World Championships and a record-breaking 65 pole positions.

Beyond his driving prowess, Senna's impact extends to his influence on the sport's ethos. He embodied a certain spirit, a relentless pursuit of excellence and a deep respect for the sport that went beyond mere competition. His commitment to fair play, his willingness to admit mistakes, and his unwavering belief in the pursuit of perfection set him apart as a role model, inspiring countless young drivers to push their boundaries and strive for greatness.

Senna's legacy goes beyond his accomplishments on the track. His charisma and his ability to connect with fans on an emotional level transcended geographical boundaries. His struggles against political oppression in his native Brazil, his outspoken stance against injustice, and his philanthropic endeavors resonated with people around the world, solidifying his image as a champion for social justice. . .

Senna's tragedy, the crash that ended his life at the 1994 San Marino Grand Prix, was met with an outpouring of grief that extended far beyond the racing community. The world mourned the loss of a sporting icon, a humanitarian, and a symbol of hope. His passing was not just the end of a racing career; it was the silencing of a powerful voice for social change.

Despite his untimely demise, Senna's legacy continues to inspire. His commitment to excellence, his passion for racing, and his unwavering spirit serve as a guiding light for aspiring drivers and athletes alike. His humanitarian efforts, his unwavering belief in the power of sport to bring people together, and his fight for social justice continue to resonate with generations of fans and social activists.

Senna's impact on the world of motorsports is undeniable. He transformed the way the sport was perceived, pushing boundaries, demanding excellence, and redefining what it meant to be a champion. But his impact goes far beyond the racetrack. He embodies the power of human spirit, the unwavering pursuit of dreams, and the belief that one individual can make a difference. This is the true essence of Ayrton Senna's legacy, a lasting testament to a man who lived and raced with passion, courage, and a profound love for the sport he dedicated his life to.

Posthumous honors and tributes

Ayrton Senna's untimely death on May 1st, 1994, at the San Marino Grand Prix, sent shockwaves through the world of motorsport and beyond. His legacy transcended the racetrack, leaving an indelible mark on hearts and minds, inspiring generations to come. His passing ignited a wave of grief and disbelief, but also a fervent desire to commemorate the extraordinary talent and humanitarian spirit that defined the Brazilian driver. The outpouring of love and admiration from fans, fellow drivers, and even world leaders underscored the profound impact he had made on the global stage.

The tributes began almost immediately, with the racing community coming together to pay their respects. The Formula One circus, momentarily stunned into silence, reeled from the loss of their star. The Brazilian flag flew at half-mast at circuits around the world, a symbolic gesture of shared mourning. Fellow drivers, many of whom had competed alongside Senna, spoke of their profound loss, sharing anecdotes of his unwavering dedication, competitive spirit, and genuine warmth. The legend of Ayrton Senna was born not just on the track, but in the hearts of those he touched.

Beyond the racetrack, tributes poured in from all corners of the globe. Governments and world leaders offered condolences, acknowledging Senna's impact as a global icon and his influence on a generation. The Brazilian people, deeply proud of their national hero, mourned his loss with a collective outpouring of grief. His funeral was a monumental event, a sea of mourners filling the streets of São Paulo, their sorrow a testament to his enduring legacy.

The years following his death saw a steady stream of commemorations and tributes. Museums and foundations dedicated to his memory were established, meticulously preserving his legacy and sharing his story with future generations. His iconic helmet, a symbol of his fearless spirit, became a cherished artifact, showcased in exhibitions and museums worldwide. The Ayrton Senna Institute, founded by his family, embodies his humanitarian spirit, focusing on education and social development for underprivileged children in Brazil, carrying forward his unwavering belief in the transformative power of education.

The impact of Ayrton Senna on motorsport is immeasurable. His driving style, a masterful blend of precision, aggression, and unwavering focus, redefined the sport. His innovative approach to race strategy and technical development pushed the boundaries of engineering and performance, influencing generations of drivers and engineers. His legacy transcends the technical aspects of racing, inspiring generations with his unwavering commitment to excellence, his unmatched talent, and his profound spirit.

His dedication to his craft, his unwavering pursuit of perfection, and his humanitarian spirit continue to inspire. He became a global icon, not just for his achievements on the track, but for the positive impact he had on the world. His legacy lives on through his foundation, his fans, and the countless individuals who draw inspiration from his life and work. The 1994 San Marino Grand Prix, a day etched in motorsport history, stands as a poignant reminder of the tragic loss of a racing legend. However, it also serves as a testament to the enduring legacy of a man who transcended the sport and left an indelible mark on the world. .

.

Chapter 6: Beyond the Track

Senna's activism and humanitarian efforts

Beyond the roar of the engines and the blur of speed, Ayrton Senna possessed a profound empathy for the human condition. His activism and humanitarian efforts transcended the world of motorsports, revealing a soul deeply committed to social justice and human betterment. This commitment wasn't a fleeting fad, but a deeply ingrained principle that guided his actions, his words, and his life. .

Senna's advocacy was often expressed through his unwavering support for the Instituto Ayrton Senna (IAS), a foundation he established in 1994, a year before his tragic death. The IAS, a testament to his belief in education as a catalyst for social change, sought to empower disadvantaged children in Brazil through educational programs. Its core objective was to equip children with the tools and opportunities to break the cycle of poverty, fostering a brighter future for generations to come.

Senna's commitment to the IAS wasn't a mere gesture; it was a personal calling. He dedicated a significant portion of his wealth and time to the foundation, meticulously overseeing its operations and actively participating in fundraising initiatives. He believed in the power of education to unlock potential, transforming lives and fostering a more equitable society.

Beyond the IAS, Senna's humanitarian efforts manifested in various ways. His unwavering support for UNICEF, the United Nations Children's Fund, reflected his deeply held conviction in protecting children's rights and ensuring their well-being. He used his platform as a global icon to advocate for children's rights, raising awareness about issues such as poverty, malnutrition, and lack of access to education.

Senna's humanitarianism extended beyond specific organizations. He was known for his generous donations to various charities and his unwavering willingness to lend a helping hand to those in need. Whether it was supporting a local orphanage or providing financial assistance to struggling families, Senna's compassion and generosity knew no bounds.

His activism transcended mere philanthropy, extending into the realm of social change. He used his influence to champion social justice issues, speaking out against racial discrimination, advocating for environmental protection, and promoting peace and understanding. He wasn't afraid to use his voice to address sensitive topics, even when it went against the grain of public opinion.

The 1992 Brazilian Grand Prix, a race marred by controversy, serves as a poignant example of Senna's courage and conviction. Despite the intense pressure and scrutiny, he refused to participate in a staged finish, a blatant attempt to manipulate the race outcome for political gain. His stance, a testament to his unwavering integrity, highlighted his commitment to fair play and ethical conduct.

Senna's actions and words carried profound significance. They resonated with people from all walks of life, inspiring countless individuals to follow his example. His legacy as a champion for humanity endures, his commitment to social justice, and his unwavering pursuit of a better world continue to inspire generations.

Senna's humanitarian work was not just about charity, but about creating a tangible impact. He understood the complexities of social issues and sought practical solutions. He believed in empowering communities through education, promoting social inclusion, and tackling inequality at its root. His dedication to these causes was unwavering, even when faced with resistance or criticism.

His approach to humanitarian work wasn't solely about money and resources; it was about personal engagement and a genuine desire to make a difference. He saw social justice as a personal responsibility, not just a philanthropic duty. He interacted with the people he sought to help, understanding their struggles and aspirations firsthand. This genuine connection fostered a sense of trust and respect, strengthening the impact of his efforts.

His commitment to his homeland, Brazil, was deeply personal. He saw the social injustices within his country and worked tirelessly to improve the lives of the less fortunate. The IAS, his most significant contribution, embodied this commitment, aiming to empower disadvantaged children and equip them with the tools to break free from the cycle of poverty.

Beyond the tangible impact of his actions, Senna's legacy lies in the inspiration he provided. He showed the world that it's possible to be a champion on the track and a champion for humanity. He proved that athletic prowess could be coupled with compassion and social conscience. His story reminds us that even the most successful individuals can make a difference, leaving a legacy that extends far beyond their accomplishments.

Senna's activism and humanitarian efforts were a testament to his character, his values, and his commitment to a better world. They reveal a depth of compassion, integrity, and courage that transcended the world of motorsports. His legacy serves as a constant reminder that true greatness lies not just in achieving personal success but in using that success to benefit others and create a positive impact on the world.

Advocacy for safety improvements in motorsport

Ayrton Senna's influence on the world of motorsport goes far beyond his unparalleled driving skills and the iconic victories he achieved. His relentless pursuit of perfection, his fierce determination, and his unwavering passion for the sport were all hallmarks of his career, but it was his unwavering commitment to safety that cemented his legacy as an advocate for change. He saw motorsport as a dangerous endeavor, yes, but one that could be made safer with the right approach. This belief fueled his relentless drive to push for improvements, even when faced with resistance and skepticism from the establishment. .

Senna's advocacy was born from personal experience. He witnessed firsthand the dangers of motorsport, losing close friends and fellow drivers to accidents. He understood the human cost of the sport, and he refused to accept that such tragedies were simply an inevitable part of the game. He actively challenged the status quo, advocating for improved safety standards, demanding stricter regulations, and pushing for technological innovations that could protect drivers. He recognized that safety was not a matter of luck, but a matter of conscious effort. .

His advocacy manifested itself in numerous ways. He was a vocal critic of the FIA's lack of action on safety issues, often publicly challenging their decisions and advocating for stricter regulations. He pushed for the adoption of new safety technologies, like HANS devices, which help to prevent head and neck injuries. He championed the development of safer circuits, advocating for increased runoff areas, barrier improvements, and better medical infrastructure. He was a constant presence in the safety commission, actively participating in discussions and contributing to the development of new regulations. .

Senna's impact was not just limited to pushing for regulations and technological advancements. He also became a powerful voice for driver safety awareness. He understood the importance of educating drivers about the inherent dangers of the sport, emphasizing the need for careful driving, risk assessment, and a respect for the limits of the car and the track. He instilled in young drivers a sense of responsibility, encouraging them to prioritize safety alongside speed.

Senna's advocacy, however, was not without its challenges. He faced resistance from some who saw his push for safety as a hindrance to the excitement of the sport. Some argued that his focus on safety would slow down the racing and compromise the thrill of the competition. Others felt that the sport's inherent danger was part of its appeal, and that making it safer would diminish its allure. .

Senna, however, remained unwavering in his commitment to safety. He believed that safety was not a contradiction to the thrill of racing, but rather an essential ingredient in making the sport more sustainable and allowing it to thrive for generations to come. He viewed it as a responsibility, a moral imperative, and a testament to the respect he held for the drivers and the sport itself. .

Senna's tragic death in 1994 was a stark reminder of the dangers of the sport, but it also solidified his legacy as a champion of safety. His advocacy for improved safety standards had a lasting impact on the sport, leading to significant advancements in the years following his death. Many of the safety features that are now commonplace in motorsport, from HANS devices to improved safety barriers, were either directly inspired by Senna's efforts or were the result of the renewed focus on safety that he brought to the forefront.

Senna's legacy as an advocate for safety in motorsport is a testament to his unwavering commitment to the sport and its participants. His fierce determination to improve safety standards and his tireless efforts to educate drivers and push for better regulations have had a lasting impact on the sport, making it safer and ensuring that future generations of drivers can compete in a sport that prioritizes safety while still retaining the thrill of racing. His legacy is not just about his victories on the track, but about his enduring impact on the sport's evolution and his dedication to protecting the lives of those who participate in it.

Chapter 7: Technical Prowess

Senna's innovative driving style and exceptional car control

Ayrton Senna's legacy transcends mere victory; it embodies an unparalleled symbiosis between man and machine, a relationship forged through innovation and an almost supernatural control over the limits of physics. His driving style, far from conventional, defied categorization. It was a tapestry of daring, finesse, and unwavering focus, woven with a thread of intuitive understanding that bordered on telepathic communication with the car. .

Senna didn't simply drive; he danced with the machine, feeling its every nuance, anticipating its every twitch. His steering inputs, while precise and controlled, were often unorthodox. Instead of the smooth, flowing movements preferred by many, Senna's steering was punctuated by short, sharp adjustments, seemingly wrestling the car through corners with a blend of audacity and meticulousness. This technique, bordering on a ballet of the steering wheel, allowed him to extract the maximum grip from the car's tires, finding a delicate balance on the edge of adhesion. .

The key to Senna's mastery lay in his understanding of the car's behavior, not just in terms of its mechanical intricacies, but also its inherent limitations. He could sense the point where the car was about to break free, where the tires would lose grip, and he would anticipate those moments with remarkable precision. This knowledge was not derived from theory; it was born from countless hours spent pushing the car to its absolute limits, learning its strengths and weaknesses in a way that transcended the limitations of data and telemetry.

This understanding translated into his braking, which was equally unconventional. Senna was known for his late, aggressive braking, a technique that seemed to defy the laws of physics. But it was this daring strategy that allowed him to outbrake his rivals, generating a crucial advantage in the braking zone and setting him up for a superior exit from the corner. It was not just about the pressure applied to the brake pedal; it was about the timing, the finesse, and the ability to modulate the braking force to maximize grip and maintain control.

His signature move, the "Senna slide," epitomized his exceptional control over the car. This maneuver, executed at the limit of adhesion, involved a controlled oversteer into a corner, allowing him to maintain speed and carve a path through the apex, seemingly defying the laws of physics. It was a demonstration of his profound understanding of the car's dynamics, a calculated risk that only someone with absolute trust in their abilities could execute.

Senna's driving style was not about brute force; it was about finesse and intelligence. He was a master of anticipating the car's behavior, predicting its responses, and adjusting his inputs with a level of precision that seemed almost instinctive. It was a symphony of movement, a dance between man and machine, driven by an unwavering focus and a profound connection with the car that few could match.

This masterful control extended beyond the racetrack. Senna possessed a unique ability to communicate with his engineers, conveying his feedback in a precise and nuanced manner. He could pinpoint the subtle nuances of the car's handling, detailing the slightest imbalance, the smallest change in grip, and expressing his needs in a way that allowed the engineers to understand his perspective and optimize the car's performance.

Senna's legacy extends far beyond his championship trophies and record-breaking wins. His driving style, his innovative approach, and his profound connection with the machines he piloted redefined the art of driving. It was a testament to his unparalleled skill, his unwavering focus, and his ability to push the boundaries of what was considered possible, leaving an indelible mark on the world of motorsports. He was not just a driver; he was a maestro, conducting a symphony of speed and precision, forever etched in the annals of racing history.

Contributions to advancements in Formula 1 technology

While Ayrton Senna is primarily remembered for his unparalleled driving skill, his contributions to Formula 1 technology are often overshadowed. His relentless pursuit of perfection, coupled with a keen understanding of car dynamics and a relentless drive to push the boundaries of engineering, resulted in significant advancements that shaped the sport and continue to influence it today. .

Senna's influence on F1 technology can be traced to his early years with Toleman and Lotus, where he actively engaged with engineers, providing crucial feedback and insights that helped develop innovative solutions. His ability to feel the car's limits and communicate these nuances to the engineers allowed them to refine and improve the car's performance. This collaborative approach fostered a culture of innovation within the teams, as engineers were encouraged to experiment and push the limits of what was possible.

One of Senna's most notable contributions was his advocacy for active suspension systems. In an era dominated by passive suspension, Senna's feedback and detailed descriptions of car behavior during cornering and braking convinced the Lotus team to invest in active suspension technology. This groundbreaking system, pioneered by Lotus, revolutionized F1, allowing cars to adapt to different track conditions and improve handling and cornering speeds. Senna's relentless pursuit of every possible advantage, coupled with his precise feedback, played a crucial role in accelerating the development and adoption of this transformative technology. .

Senna's understanding of tire behavior and his ability to extract maximum grip from the tires was legendary. He would often push the limits of tire performance, providing the engineers with invaluable data that helped them develop tires with better grip and durability. This collaboration between Senna and the engineers at Goodyear resulted in the development of tires with a wider operating window and better grip, especially in wet conditions, which contributed significantly to his dominance in rain-affected races.

Senna's influence extended beyond technical advancements to the development of driving techniques. His mastery of car control, particularly in challenging conditions, inspired a generation of drivers to adopt a more aggressive and precise approach to driving. His use of techniques like trail braking and late apexing, combined with his extraordinary ability to manage tire wear, became the standard in the sport, elevating the level of driving and pushing the limits of car performance. .

While Senna's untimely passing in 1994 cut short his career, his legacy continues to inspire engineers and drivers alike. His passion for pushing the boundaries of technology, his collaborative approach to engineering, and his unwavering commitment to excellence continue to influence the sport today. Senna's contributions to F1 technology extend far beyond his victories and accolades; he played a pivotal role in shaping the sport's trajectory, ushering in a new era of innovation and pushing the limits of performance on and off the track. His impact on F1 engineering and driving techniques remains evident in every race, as drivers and engineers continue to strive for excellence and innovation, echoing the spirit of the legendary Brazilian champion.

Chapter 8: Psychological Warfare

Senna's mental fortitude and competitive edge

Ayrton Senna, the name echoes with a thunderous roar, a legacy built not just on speed and skill, but on an iron will that forged him into a racing icon. His competitive edge wasn't solely reliant on the horsepower under the hood, but on the unyielding mental strength that fueled his relentless pursuit of victory. His mental fortitude, a cornerstone of his legacy, transcended the racetrack, manifesting as a driving force in his life and resonating with fans across the globe. .

Senna's mental resilience was not an innate trait, but a honed weapon, meticulously sharpened through years of dedicated practice and unwavering focus. He recognized that the mental game was as crucial as physical prowess, and thus embraced a relentless regimen to cultivate his inner strength. His commitment to visualizing success, meticulously analyzing race strategies, and relentlessly pushing his physical and mental limits fueled a mental fortitude that propelled him to greatness. This unwavering determination extended beyond the race track, permeating his personal life and shaping his unwavering pursuit of excellence in every aspect of his being.

His mental tenacity was a constant companion, an unflinching force that enabled him to face adversity with unwavering resolve. The crucible of competition, fraught with immense pressure and relentless scrutiny, became a breeding ground for his mental fortitude. The roar of the crowd, the pressure of expectations, the relentless pursuit of victory - all these elements, far from overwhelming him, served as fuel for his inner fire. He embraced the challenge, using it as a springboard to elevate his performance.

The mental fortitude that defined Senna's competitive edge was not merely a matter of resilience but also of calculated aggression. He understood the psychology of racing, the intricate interplay of confidence, intimidation, and psychological warfare. He used this understanding to his advantage, projecting an aura of unwavering confidence that often disarmed his opponents. This calculated aggression wasn't a display of bravado, but a strategic maneuver, a silent weapon in his arsenal of mental dominance.

Senna's strategic brilliance extended beyond the racetrack, translating into a masterful understanding of the psychological nuances of competition. He recognized the power of intimidation and employed it with calculated precision, creating a mental landscape where his rivals were forced to operate on his terms. His unwavering confidence became a tangible presence, a silent force that influenced the mental state of his competitors, often tipping the balance in his favor.

His fierce determination and relentless pursuit of perfection created a mental landscape that resonated with his fans, who saw in him a reflection of their own aspirations. They recognized the unwavering resolve that fueled his relentless pursuit of victory, an unwavering commitment that transcended the realm of sport and resonated with a deeper human yearning for excellence.

Senna's mental fortitude wasn't just about the victories he achieved, but about the legacy he left behind. His unwavering commitment to pushing boundaries, his relentless pursuit of perfection, and his unwavering belief in himself inspired generations of drivers and fans alike. His mental strength, a testament to his unwavering dedication and relentless pursuit of greatness, remains an enduring legacy, a testament to the profound impact of mental fortitude on human achievement.

Use of on-track mind games and aggression

Ayrton Senna, the Brazilian Formula One legend, was more than just a brilliant driver. He was a master of the mental game, using psychological warfare to gain an edge over his rivals. This wasn't about intimidation or brute force; it was about understanding the opponent's psyche and exploiting their weaknesses to create opportunities for himself. Senna's on-track aggression was not simply a byproduct of his natural competitiveness, but a carefully calculated strategy that often involved a delicate dance of psychological manipulation. .

Senna's understanding of the human element in racing was evident in his choice of tactics. He would often use psychological warfare to unsettle his rivals, throwing them off their game and forcing them into mistakes. A classic example is his 1990 Hungarian Grand Prix victory. Leading the race, Senna was challenged by Alain Prost. To deter Prost from trying an overtake, Senna held him up for several laps, forcing the Frenchman into frustration and ultimately causing him to make a mistake that lost him valuable time. The frustration on Prost's face was palpable, and the victory, while hard-earned, was a testament to Senna's ability to manipulate his opponent's emotions. .

Senna's tactics went beyond just driving aggressively. His ability to read his opponents' weaknesses, both on and off the track, gave him a strategic advantage. In qualifying sessions, he often utilized psychological warfare to unsettle rivals, creating a sense of pressure and uncertainty. He understood the importance of psychological dominance in qualifying, as it often gave him a crucial head start in the race. His ability to project an aura of confidence and determination, even when facing pressure, further contributed to his psychological advantage. .

The intensity of his rivalry with Alain Prost, one of the greatest drivers of all time, highlighted Senna's use of psychological warfare. Their duels were often fierce and dramatic, with both drivers pushing each other to the limit. While Prost's approach was characterized by calm and calculated aggression, Senna relied more on aggressive tactics and mental manipulation. He would often use psychological games, like deliberately braking late or making sudden moves, to unsettle Prost and force errors. .

Senna's aggressive driving style, often perceived as reckless by some, was a key part of his psychological warfare. While it could be intimidating, it also served as a way to establish dominance and send a clear message to his rivals. He wasn't afraid to take risks, knowing that his opponents would often hesitate to match his level of aggression. This aggressive style became his signature, his weapon of choice in the mental battle on the track.

His on-track aggression, however, wasn't simply about intimidation or bravado. It was a carefully crafted strategy to disrupt his opponents' rhythm, causing them to make mistakes and granting him the opportunity to capitalize on their errors. His ability to maintain focus and drive with relentless intensity even under pressure, became his mental edge. .

Senna's tactics weren't always welcomed by his opponents. He was often criticized for his aggressive driving and the psychological games he played. However, his opponents couldn't deny his brilliance and the effectiveness of his tactics. His approach was, in its own way, a testament to his deep understanding of the mental aspects of racing and his ability to use them to his advantage. .

Senna's on-track battles were not just about physical skill; they were a microcosm of human psychology, a testament to his understanding of the mental game. His legacy is not just about his driving skills, but about his mastery of psychological warfare, his ability to leverage his opponent's emotions and weaknesses to create an advantage. This is a critical element of Senna's legacy, a dimension often overlooked in the narratives of his brilliance. The psychological battle was as important to his success as the physical one, and it is an element that continues to fascinate and inspire, even years after his tragic passing.

Chapter 9: Controversies and Rivalries

Notable incidents and confrontations

The story of Ayrton Senna is woven with threads of unparalleled skill, fierce determination, and undeniable charisma. However, it is also marked by numerous controversies and rivalries that fueled his legend and, at times, cast a shadow over his achievements. .

One of the most prominent and enduring rivalries in motorsport history unfolded between Senna and his fellow Brazilian, Nelson Piquet. Theirs was a complex dynamic, fueled by contrasting personalities and ambitions. While Senna was driven by a relentless pursuit of perfection, Piquet possessed a more calculated, opportunistic approach. Their relationship was marked by moments of mutual respect, punctuated by bitter confrontations. .

A key incident occurred during the 1987 San Marino Grand Prix. Senna, driving for Lotus, found himself locked in a fierce battle with Piquet, then at the wheel of a Williams. As they navigated a tight corner, Senna, with his trademark precision, squeezed Piquet into the barriers, forcing him to spin out. This incident, which raised questions about Senna's sporting etiquette, ignited a firestorm of controversy. .

However, it was during the 1990 Japanese Grand Prix that their rivalry reached its peak. Senna, by now a dominant force in Formula One, was leading the race when his engine stalled. This sudden setback propelled Piquet into the lead, offering him a chance to win his third world championship. However, in a controversial maneuver, Piquet ignored team orders and intentionally slowed the pace of the race, preventing his teammate, Alain Prost, from catching up. This calculated move, seemingly designed to secure his own championship triumph, further escalated the feud between Senna and Piquet.

Yet, it was Alain Prost, the French driving maestro, who became the ultimate symbol of Senna's rivalries. Their relationship, despite initial mutual respect, evolved into a heated battle for supremacy, fueled by clashes on the track and off. .

The 1989 Japanese Grand Prix epitomized this contentious rivalry. With both drivers vying for the world championship, the race unfolded under the shadow of intense pressure. At the infamous Suzuka corner, Senna attempted a daring overtake, leaving Prost stranded on the outside. The two cars collided, with Senna emerging victorious. However, the incident led to accusations of deliberate foul play, casting a long shadow over Senna's triumph. .

The following year, at the same circuit, the drama escalated. Senna, determined to reclaim the championship, engaged in a tactical maneuver, leading to a collision with Prost at the start of the race. This controversial move, which ultimately ended in a disqualification for Senna, cemented the intensity of their rivalry and highlighted the ethical complexities of their competition. .

These incidents, fueled by a potent combination of ambition, talent, and conflicting personalities, shaped the narrative of Senna's career, and ultimately, his legacy. They reveal a side of the driver, often veiled beneath his impeccable skill and magnetic charisma, showcasing the depths of his competitive spirit, his unwavering determination, and his willingness to push the boundaries of sportsmanship in his relentless pursuit of victory. .

The confrontations, while often marred by accusations of unsporting behavior, also served as a testament to Senna's extraordinary talent and unwavering commitment. They underlined the intensity of the Formula One world, a world where every driver, regardless of their status, is ultimately pitted against each other, vying for the same coveted prize. .

In the end, Senna's legacy remains a complex tapestry, woven with threads of brilliance, controversy, and captivating rivalry. His confrontations, while serving as reminders of the fierce competitiveness of the sport, also serve as a testament to the impact of his talent and the enduring legacy of a driver who dared to push the limits, leaving an indelible mark on the history of motorsport.

Rivalry with Alain Prost

The rivalry between Ayrton Senna and Alain Prost, two titans of Formula One racing, transcended the boundaries of mere competition and became a defining chapter in the sport's history. Their clash on the track, fueled by contrasting personalities and driving styles, captivated the world and ultimately left an enduring mark on the legacy of both drivers. .

Senna, the relentless, fearless Brazilian, possessed a fiery spirit that burned with an unyielding thirst for victory. His driving was characterized by an aggressive, almost cavalier, approach, pushing the limits of both car and driver to the absolute edge. He was a master of overtaking, his daring maneuvers often leaving his rivals in awe and occasionally, in a state of disbelief. Prost, the cerebral Frenchman, was the epitome of precision and tactical brilliance. He approached the sport with a calculated, methodical approach, meticulously analyzing every detail and leaving nothing to chance. His driving was characterized by smoothness and finesse, a testament to his exceptional talent and unwavering focus.

Their contrasting personalities and driving styles set the stage for an inevitable clash. In the early stages of their rivalry, a mutual respect existed, but as their paths continued to cross, the battle for supremacy escalated. Their first encounter on the podium at the 1984 San Marino Grand Prix, where Senna famously celebrated his victory by mimicking Prost's signature salute, foreshadowed the intensity of their future battles. .

The 1988 season, Senna's first year with McLaren, marked the beginning of their most intense rivalry. Senna's dominance, coupled with Prost's determination to retain his championship title, fueled a palpable tension between the two drivers. At the Japanese Grand Prix, the first real turning point in their rivalry, Senna's aggressive overtaking maneuver forced Prost off the track. The incident sparked a wave of controversy, with accusations of foul play thrown back and forth. .

The 1989 season continued the bitter rivalry, escalating to a dramatic climax at the Japanese Grand Prix. The pre-race press conference was filled with heated exchanges, with Senna refusing to shake Prost's hand. During the race, Prost, seeking to secure the championship, attempted a tactical maneuver by yielding the lead to Senna, believing that his teammate would follow suit. Senna, however, had other plans and proceeded to pass Prost, ultimately winning the race. .

The incident sparked accusations of deliberate sabotage, fueling the flames of their rivalry. The resulting controversy overshadowed the championship victory, leaving a stain on the sport's integrity. The 1990 season saw their rivalry reach a boiling point at the Japanese Grand Prix. Senna's collision with Prost in the first corner, which many viewed as an intentional attempt to take Prost out of the race, solidified the animosity that had festered between the two drivers. The incident led to Prost's retirement, leaving Senna to win the championship in a deeply controversial manner.

Their rivalry, however, went beyond the track. The media frenzy surrounding their clashes fuelled a public perception of animosity and betrayal. The press often painted them as arch-enemies, their every move dissected and analyzed. While it's true that their rivalry was marked by tense moments and bitter exchanges, it's important to remember that their interactions extended beyond the rivalry, encompassing a shared passion for the sport and a deep understanding of each other's strengths and weaknesses. .

The rivalry between Senna and Prost, though often acrimonious, ultimately enriched the sport of Formula One. It captivated audiences, raising the stakes and pushing the boundaries of competition. It provided fans with a thrilling spectacle, one that continues to be discussed and debated even today. .

Senna and Prost, despite their differences, were both undisputed legends of the sport. Their rivalry, though intense, served as a testament to their extraordinary talent and unwavering determination. Their legacy, forever intertwined, continues to inspire and challenge generations of racing enthusiasts, leaving an indelible mark on the history of Formula One. The rivalry, while steeped in controversy, ultimately reflected the competitive spirit of the sport, pushing both drivers to new heights of excellence..

.

Chapter 10: The Human Side

Senna's personality, values, and personal relationships

Ayrton Senna, the name evokes an immediate image - a fiery, relentless driver who dominated the world of Formula One racing. His driving style, characterized by unmatched precision and a fierce competitive spirit, cemented his place as a legend. But beyond the helmet and the roar of the engine, lay a man deeply rooted in his values, his relationships, and a personality that transcended the realm of sports.

Senna's personality was an intricate tapestry woven from a blend of passion, dedication, and a profound respect for his craft. He was a man driven by an unyielding desire for perfection, both on and off the track. His meticulous approach to racing extended to every aspect of his life. He meticulously analyzed data, meticulously prepared for each race, and meticulously strived for excellence in everything he undertook. This meticulousness was not a mere obsession with perfection; it was a testament to his deep-seated belief in giving his best, in pushing his limits, in leaving nothing to chance. This relentless pursuit of excellence, coupled with his intense focus, often led to the perception of him as a demanding and even intimidating figure. However, beneath this outward appearance lay a man of immense sensitivity and compassion. This duality in his personality, his unwavering determination juxtaposed with his deep empathy, was a defining characteristic of his being.

Senna's values were deeply ingrained in his upbringing and his Brazilian heritage. His family instilled in him a strong sense of faith, a belief in God's presence, and a commitment to integrity. These values were not merely abstract concepts; they were the bedrock upon which he built his life. His faith provided him with solace and strength, particularly during the challenging moments of his racing career. His belief in integrity guided his actions, both on and off the track, making him a champion who fiercely defended his principles. He shunned any form of deceit or manipulation, upholding the spirit of fair play, even in the fiercely competitive world of Formula One. This unwavering adherence to his values, his commitment to integrity and fairness, distinguished him as a man of character, a true champion in every sense of the word.

Senna's relationships were the foundation of his life, providing him with unwavering support and a sense of belonging. His family played a pivotal role in shaping his values and nurturing his passion for racing. His father, Milton da Silva, was his mentor and confidante, providing him with unwavering support throughout his racing career. His mother, Neyde, instilled in him a deep sense of compassion and empathy, qualities that shone through in his interactions with others. His sister, Viviane, served as his anchor, his confidante, and his constant source of strength. The close-knit bonds within his family, the unwavering love and support they provided, were crucial in navigating the demanding world of professional racing, a world filled with pressure and relentless scrutiny. .

Beyond his immediate family, Senna's relationships extended to his colleagues and fellow drivers. He formed deep friendships with several of his competitors, including Alain Prost, with whom he shared a passionate rivalry on the track. Despite their on-track rivalry, they developed a deep respect for each other's abilities and shared a mutual admiration for each other's skills. These friendships, forged in the crucible of intense competition, highlighted the human side of Senna, a side often overlooked by those who only saw the champion on the track. .

Senna's relationships were not confined to the realm of racing. He was known for his philanthropy, his commitment to helping those in need, particularly in his native Brazil. His foundation, the Instituto Ayrton Senna, established to provide educational opportunities for underprivileged children, was a testament to his deep compassion and desire to make a positive impact on the world. This commitment to helping others, to making a difference beyond the world of racing, demonstrated the depth of his humanity, his desire to leave a legacy that extended beyond the chequered flag.

It reveals a man who was deeply rooted in his values, a man who fiercely defended his principles, a man who valued relationships above all else, and a man whose compassion extended beyond the racetrack. Senna's personality, his values, and his relationships were the pillars upon which he built his life, and they were the driving force behind his enduring legacy. He wasn't just a champion on the track; he was a champion in life, a man who lived his values, who nurtured his relationships, and who left an indelible mark on the world. .

.

Struggles and triumphs off the track

Ayrton Senna, the name synonymous with speed, precision, and unparalleled skill on the racetrack, was also a man grappling with profound personal struggles and triumphs that extended far beyond the roar of engines and the checkered flag. Beneath the helmet and the racing suit, a complex and multifaceted human being resided, driven by an unyielding pursuit of excellence, but also burdened by anxieties, fears, and a deep-seated sense of responsibility. .

Senna's upbringing in Sao Paulo, Brazil, amidst the political and economic turmoil of the 1970s, shaped him into a man of immense conviction and a strong sense of justice. His family's financial struggles and the turbulent times fostered a determination to overcome obstacles and achieve his dreams. This inherent resilience fueled his relentless pursuit of success in motorsport, but it also created a deep-seated anxiety about failure, a constant fear of letting down those who believed in him. .

The pressure of being a national hero, carrying the hopes and dreams of an entire nation on his shoulders, was immense. The weight of expectation, the burden of being a symbol of Brazilian pride, constantly weighed on him. Every race, every performance, became a referendum on his ability to deliver, to live up to the image projected onto him. This pressure manifested itself in his intense focus, his unwavering determination, and a relentless drive to push himself beyond his perceived limits. .

However, Senna's struggles were not confined to the racetrack. He carried a deep-seated melancholy, a sense of loneliness that stemmed from the relentless pursuit of his passion. He was a man who dedicated his life to racing, sacrificing personal relationships, emotional attachments, and a sense of normalcy in his quest for glory. While his devotion to the sport brought him immense success and adulation, it also left him yearning for something more, a sense of belonging and connection beyond the realm of high-octane competition. .

His personal relationships often suffered from the demands of his career. The pressure to perform, the constant travel, and the all-consuming nature of his pursuit left little room for meaningful connections. His marriages, though passionate, were ultimately marked by the same intensity and drive that defined his approach to racing, resulting in their eventual dissolution. This constant pursuit of excellence, of pushing himself to the limit, often came at the expense of his personal life, leaving him feeling isolated and alone despite the cheers of the crowd and the adulation of his fans.

Yet, amidst the struggles, triumphs emerged. Senna's legacy transcends the victories and the world championships. He became a symbol of resilience, a testament to the power of determination and unwavering focus. His unwavering commitment to his craft, his refusal to settle for anything less than excellence, inspired millions around the world. He was a beacon of hope, a symbol of the human spirit's ability to overcome adversity and achieve the seemingly impossible. .

His philanthropy, often overlooked amidst the roar of the engines, further highlighted his compassionate nature. He dedicated significant time and resources to supporting children in need, particularly those facing poverty and hardship. His charitable endeavors, though often conducted with a quiet humility, showcased a side of him that contrasted sharply with the fierce competitor seen on the racetrack. This act of giving, of reaching out to those less fortunate, provided a sense of purpose and fulfillment that transcended the materialistic nature of his profession. .

The tragic accident that ended his life on the track in 1994 sent shockwaves around the world. His sudden passing left a void in the sport, a sense of loss that reverberated through the hearts of millions. But beyond the tragedy, Senna's legacy continues to inspire. He was a man who lived and breathed racing, but his story is a testament to the human spirit's capacity for perseverance, resilience, and compassion. .

Senna's struggles and triumphs off the track are a reminder that behind the mask of the racing icon, a complex and multifaceted human being existed. He was a man driven by ambition, haunted by fears, and yet deeply compassionate and committed to making a positive impact on the world. His life, though tragically cut short, serves as an enduring reminder that even the greatest champions are not immune to the complexities and contradictions inherent in the human experience. .

.

Chapter 11: The Legend Lives On

Senna's enduring popularity and cultural impact

Ayrton Senna, the Brazilian Formula One driver, transcended the realm of mere motorsport champion to become a global icon, his legacy resonating through the decades. His enduring popularity transcends mere sporting achievement, reflecting a complex interplay of factors that cemented his place as a cultural phenomenon. Senna's impact lies in his captivating driving style, his inherent charisma, his tragic demise, and the profound connection he forged with his fans. .

Senna's driving, a blend of audacious aggression and calculated precision, was a spectacle in itself. His signature "Senna slide," a masterful maneuver employing throttle control and steering precision to navigate corners, became a symbol of his daring. Witnessing him at the apex of a corner, pushing the limits of both car and driver, was an experience that captivated audiences. This exhilarating spectacle, coupled with his consistent dominance in the sport, propelled him to the forefront of Formula One, solidifying his position as a racing deity.

Beyond the racetrack, Senna possessed an undeniable charisma. His determination, unwavering focus, and uncompromising pursuit of excellence resonated with millions. His intensity, both on and off the track, was palpable, fueling a fervent admiration and loyalty among his followers. While his rivals, like Alain Prost, embodied a cool, calculated approach to the sport, Senna's raw emotion, his burning desire to win, provided an irresistible narrative for fans. This passionate, human element solidified his connection with audiences, transcending the typical athlete-fan relationship.

Senna's enduring appeal is further amplified by the tragic circumstances of his death. His fatal crash at the 1994 San Marino Grand Prix, while leading the race, cemented his status as a martyr. This untimely demise, coupled with his undeniable charisma, solidified his legend. His fans, unable to reconcile with his absence, mourned his loss profoundly, elevating him to a mythical figure. This tragic end further fueled the narrative of his unwavering determination, his constant pursuit of excellence, culminating in a martyrdom that cemented his place as an icon. .

Senna's impact extends beyond the sport, influencing popular culture across various domains. His name has become synonymous with speed, precision, and ambition. His driving style, his unwavering determination, his iconic helmet, and his tragic demise have been immortalized in numerous films, documentaries, and video games. Artists, musicians, and even fashion designers have drawn inspiration from his legacy, incorporating his signature colors and motifs into their creations. .

Senna's cultural impact is further evident in the vast and vibrant fan community that continues to celebrate his legacy. Dedicated websites, forums, and fan clubs dedicated to his memory are testament to the enduring nature of his appeal. These communities, spanning the globe, perpetuate his story, sharing anecdotes, memories, and analyses of his career, ensuring that his legacy remains vibrant.

Beyond the mere sporting achievements, Senna's enduring popularity stems from the human element he projected. His passion, his dedication, and his inherent charisma, alongside his tragic demise, created a compelling narrative that resonated deeply with audiences. This potent combination, coupled with his undeniable talent and unmatched driving ability, solidified his position as a cultural icon, one whose influence continues to inspire and captivate generations. His story serves as a powerful reminder of the human spirit's ability to achieve greatness, even in the face of adversity.

Museums, memorials, and ongoing tributes

Ayrton Senna's legacy transcends the racetrack, extending into a tapestry of museums, memorials, and ongoing tributes that honor his life and achievements. His impact on motorsport is undeniable, but his influence stretches far beyond the realm of speed and adrenaline. Senna's unwavering determination, his indomitable spirit, and his unparalleled driving talent have inspired generations of drivers and fans alike. This enduring legacy is embodied in the numerous spaces and events dedicated to commemorating his memory.

The Ayrton Senna Institute, founded by his family in 1994, is a testament to his enduring spirit. This non-profit organization works to improve the lives of underprivileged children in Brazil, a cause Senna deeply believed in. Through education, health, and social programs, the Institute embodies the values of perseverance and social responsibility that defined Senna's character. It serves as a living monument to his commitment to making a difference in the world.

The Museu Ayrton Senna, located in São Paulo, Brazil, provides a comprehensive glimpse into the life and career of the legendary driver. Visitors can explore his evolution from karting prodigy to Formula One champion, immersing themselves in his incredible journey through photographs, trophies, race cars, and personal artifacts. The museum serves as a pilgrimage site for Senna enthusiasts, allowing them to connect with the man behind the helmet and delve into his personality, his passion, and his dedication to the sport.

Beyond museums, Senna's presence is felt in numerous memorials scattered across the globe. The Ayrton Senna Memorial, located at the Imola circuit in Italy, is a poignant tribute to the driver who tragically lost his life there in 1994. The memorial, featuring a bronze statue of Senna in his iconic helmet, serves as a reminder of his talent, his commitment, and the immense loss felt by the motorsport community.

The Ayrton Senna Memorial Garden, located in the heart of London, England, offers a serene space for reflection and remembrance. The garden features a bronze sculpture of Senna and a plaque commemorating his life and achievements. It serves as a place for fans and admirers to pay their respects, creating a tranquil oasis amidst the bustling city.

Beyond physical monuments, the legacy of Ayrton Senna is perpetuated through countless tributes and events. The Ayrton Senna Trophy, awarded annually to the best driver in Formula One, acknowledges the sport's greatest talent and honors the champion's memory. This prestigious award, bestowed upon drivers who embody Senna's spirit of excellence and determination, ensures his influence on the sport remains enduring.

The annual Ayrton Senna Memorial Race, held in Brazil, brings together drivers from all over the world to compete in a spirit of remembrance and admiration. This race, a testament to Senna's passion for his home country, fosters a sense of community and serves as a platform for young drivers to showcase their talent.

Senna's legacy is also celebrated in the "Senna" documentary directed by Asif Kapadia. This critically acclaimed film, released in 2010, offers a compelling portrait of the driver's life and career, highlighting his extraordinary talent, his fierce determination, and his tragic demise. Through archival footage and interviews with those who knew him best, the documentary provides a multifaceted perspective on Senna's life and legacy. .

The Ayrton Senna Foundation, based in the UK, works to promote the values of determination, perseverance, and excellence that defined Senna's life. The foundation supports projects that empower young people and foster their development, aligning with Senna's vision for a better world. It serves as a testament to his enduring influence, inspiring future generations to strive for excellence and make a positive impact on the world.

The impact of Ayrton Senna reaches beyond the boundaries of the racetrack, inspiring millions around the globe. His legacy, marked by his extraordinary talent, his unwavering determination, and his unwavering commitment to making a difference, continues to resonate through these museums, memorials, and ongoing tributes. His spirit, his passion, and his desire to push the limits of human potential continue to inspire, serving as a testament to the enduring power of a true legend.

Chapter 12: Lessons from Senna

Analysis of his driving techniques, strategies, and mindset

Ayrton Senna's driving techniques, strategies, and mindset transcended the boundaries of mere skill. He was a master of the craft, pushing the limits of both man and machine to an almost supernatural level. His driving style was defined by an unparalleled precision, a relentless pursuit of perfection, and an almost preternatural ability to anticipate the track and his opponents. This chapter, "Lessons from Senna," delves into the intricate details of his approach to racing, revealing the genius that lay beneath the legendary triumphs. .

Senna's driving techniques were characterized by a unique blend of aggression and finesse. His braking points were notoriously late, often leaving opponents flabbergasted as he squeezed through the smallest of gaps. He would carry incredible speed through corners, utilizing the entire width of the track and pushing the car to its absolute limit. This aggressive style wasn't reckless, though; it was born from a deep understanding of the car's capabilities and a precise calculation of the available space. This understanding allowed Senna to extract every ounce of performance from the car, leaving his competitors in his wake.

His strategies were equally brilliant, often defying conventional wisdom. He was a master of the overtaking maneuver, using calculated bravery to outmaneuver his opponents with audacious moves. He would meticulously study his rivals' driving styles, identifying their weaknesses and exploiting them with surgical precision. This deep understanding of the tactical landscape allowed him to anticipate his opponents' actions, effectively predicting their every move and planning his counter-strategies accordingly. .

Beyond his technical prowess, Senna's mindset was the driving force behind his success. He approached racing with an unwavering focus and an iron will. He was relentlessly determined to win, pushing himself and his car to the very edge of their capabilities. This relentless pursuit of perfection was fueled by a deep-seated competitive spirit, a burning desire to be the best. .

Senna's mental fortitude was as impressive as his physical skills. He possessed the ability to shut out external distractions, focusing solely on the task at hand. He could block out the pressure of the crowd, the roar of the engines, and the noise of the competition, allowing him to remain calm and collected even in the most intense moments. This ability to stay composed under immense pressure was crucial to his success, allowing him to make clear-headed decisions and maintain his focus throughout the race. .

The chapter further delves into his relentless pursuit of perfection, his meticulous attention to detail, and his constant desire to learn and improve. His commitment to understanding the intricacies of his craft was unwavering, fueled by a desire to extract every ounce of performance from himself and his machine. This relentless dedication to excellence was not limited to the track; it permeated every aspect of his life, driving his relentless pursuit of perfection.

Senna's driving techniques, strategies, and mindset were inextricably linked, forming a powerful synergy that propelled him to legendary status. He was a master of the craft, pushing the boundaries of what was possible and leaving an indelible mark on the world of motorsport. His legacy continues to inspire and motivate generations of drivers, a testament to his enduring impact on the sport he so dearly loved. His story, a testament to the power of human will and the pursuit of excellence, is a constant reminder that the limits of what is possible are often self-imposed.

Inspiring lessons for racers, athletes, and beyond

The legacy of Ayrton Senna transcends the roar of engines and the blur of speed. It's not just about his three Formula One World Championships or the breathtaking skill he displayed on the track. It's about the indomitable spirit, the relentless pursuit of excellence, and the unwavering dedication that defined his life.

Senna's journey wasn't a charmed one. He faced challenges, setbacks, and moments of self-doubt, yet he never faltered in his pursuit of greatness. He embraced adversity as a catalyst for growth, each failure an opportunity to refine his craft and strengthen his resolve. This unwavering determination, a hallmark of Senna's persona, serves as a poignant lesson for anyone facing their own personal battles. It's a powerful reminder that success is not a linear path, but rather a journey riddled with hurdles and setbacks, each one a chance to learn, adapt, and emerge stronger.

The book highlights Senna's relentless pursuit of perfection, his unwavering commitment to pushing the boundaries of human potential. It's a lesson that extends far beyond the racetrack, resonating with anyone striving for excellence in their chosen field. Whether it's an artist refining their technique, a writer crafting their prose, or an entrepreneur building their business, the pursuit of perfection is a constant companion. It's not about achieving absolute perfection, an elusive and unattainable goal, but about striving for constant improvement, pushing the limits of one's capabilities, and relentlessly seeking ways to refine and elevate one's craft.

Senna's dedication to understanding the nuances of his craft is another defining characteristic, a testament to the power of continuous learning. His approach wasn't just about physical prowess; it was about immersing himself in the intricacies of the car, the intricacies of the track, the nuances of strategy, and the psychology of his competitors. This tireless pursuit of knowledge translated into a profound understanding of his craft, allowing him to anticipate challenges, strategize effectively, and ultimately outmaneuver his opponents. . .

This dedication to learning underscores a fundamental truth: mastery requires a constant thirst for knowledge. Whether it's delving into research, seeking mentorship, or engaging in self-study, the pursuit of continuous learning is an essential ingredient in achieving true excellence. It's about recognizing that there is always more to learn, more to understand, and more ways to refine one's craft.

Senna's legacy is not just about individual achievements; it's about the impact he had on others, the inspiration he ignited, and the legacy he built beyond the track. His unwavering commitment to excellence, his passion for the sport, and his unwavering spirit, even in the face of adversity, resonated with people from all walks of life. This, perhaps, is the most powerful lesson of all, a testament to the enduring power of human spirit and the potential to inspire and uplift others.

The book delves into Senna's role as a mentor, his willingness to guide and support younger drivers, offering valuable advice and encouraging them to pursue their dreams. This unwavering commitment to nurturing the next generation speaks volumes about his character and his belief in the power of mentorship. It's a reminder that true success is not solely about individual achievement, but also about the ripple effect we create in the lives of others.

Senna's legacy is one of unwavering dedication, relentless pursuit of excellence, and a profound commitment to leaving a lasting impact on the world. His story serves as a potent reminder that the journey toward greatness is not solely about achieving individual success, but about the impact we leave on the world around us. It's about embracing challenges, striving for continuous improvement, inspiring those around us, and ultimately, leaving a legacy that will endure long after our time on this earth has passed.

Chapter 13: A Sporting Icon

Senna's place among the greatest athletes of all time

Ayrton Senna da Silva, the Brazilian racing driver who transcended the realm of mere motorsport and etched his name into the very fabric of sporting immortality, remains a figure shrouded in enigma and awe. He was more than just a driver; he was a force of nature, a whirlwind of raw talent, and an embodiment of competitive spirit that transcended the confines of the racetrack. To truly understand Senna's place among the greatest athletes of all time requires a nuanced understanding of his impact, not only in the realm of motorsports but also in the hearts and minds of millions worldwide.

Senna's rise to prominence coincided with a golden age of Formula One racing, a period characterized by technological advancement, fierce rivalries, and a captivating spectacle that gripped the world. Amidst this landscape, he emerged as a titan, a driver who redefined the boundaries of human potential and captured the imagination with his unparalleled brilliance and unyielding determination. He possessed an almost preternatural connection with his machines, a sixth sense that allowed him to push the limits of physics and orchestrate daring maneuvers that left his rivals in awe.

However, Senna's legacy extends beyond the mere technical brilliance of his driving. His impact transcends the tangible realm of statistics and accolades. It lies in the way he captivated the world with his unyielding spirit, his emotional intensity, and his unwavering commitment to excellence. He embodied a raw, untamed passion for racing that resonated with audiences worldwide, transcending cultural and linguistic barriers.

His driving was a symphony of precision and audacity, a mesmerizing blend of control and instinct that left spectators breathless.

His fierce rivalry with Alain Prost, the reigning champion of the era, became a captivating narrative that captivated the world. The clash between their contrasting styles, their philosophical differences, and their relentless pursuit of victory transcended the boundaries of mere sporting competition. It became a microcosm of human ambition, of the relentless pursuit of greatness, and the intoxicating power of rivalry.

Senna's tragic demise in 1994, at the peak of his career, sent shockwaves through the world. It was a loss that transcended the realm of motorsport, resonating with millions who had been captivated by his brilliance and his indomitable spirit. His untimely passing cemented his status as a sporting icon, a legend whose memory continues to inspire and captivate generations of racing enthusiasts.

Comparing Senna to other sporting titans is a task riddled with complexities. While the realms of baseball, basketball, and soccer offer their own pantheon of deities, Senna's impact transcended the limitations of any specific sport. He possessed a rare combination of technical brilliance, unwavering determination, and charismatic personality that made him a global icon. His influence extended beyond the confines of the racetrack, resonating with millions across the globe.

In the annals of sporting history, few athletes have achieved such a level of global recognition and lasting impact. Senna's legacy transcends the realm of motorsports, his name forever etched into the fabric of sporting immortality. He remains a beacon of excellence, a symbol of unwavering spirit, and an enduring testament to the transformative power of passion and dedication. He is not merely a racing driver, but a symbol of human potential, a reminder that with unwavering resolve, even the most impossible feats can be achieved. .

Senna's impact continues to reverberate through the world of motorsport. His driving style, his aggressive yet precise approach, has influenced generations of drivers. His commitment to pushing the limits of human potential has become a guiding principle for countless aspiring racers. His story serves as a testament to the power of dedication, to the belief that even in the face of adversity, triumph can be achieved.

Senna's legacy extends beyond the realm of mere competition. He stands as a symbol of the human spirit, of the relentless pursuit of excellence, and the transformative power of passion. His story inspires not only aspiring racers but also anyone who seeks to push their own boundaries, to strive for greatness, and to embrace the challenges that life presents.

To truly understand Senna's place among the greatest athletes of all time, one must look beyond the statistics, the accolades, and the trophies. It is in the hearts and minds of millions around the world where his true legacy resides. He was more than just a driver; he was a beacon of inspiration, a symbol of human potential, and a reminder that even in the face of tragedy, the indomitable spirit can prevail.

Recognition for his achievements and character

Ayrton Senna da Silva, a name etched in the annals of motorsport history, transcended the status of a mere racing driver to become an icon, a legend whose impact resonated far beyond the racetrack. His accomplishments, both on and off the track, solidified his place as one of the greatest drivers ever, but it was his unique character that truly set him apart, forging an enduring legacy that continues to inspire generations.

Senna's racing achievements speak volumes about his exceptional talent. He secured three Formula One world championships in 1988, 1990, and 1991, proving his dominance in a sport demanding unparalleled skill, precision, and mental fortitude. Beyond the championships, his record reflects a captivating blend of raw speed and tactical brilliance. His ability to push the limits of his car and his own physical and mental endurance, evident in countless victories and pole positions, solidified his reputation as a force to be reckoned with. However, it was not just the sheer number of wins that solidified Senna's legend, but the way he achieved them. His overtaking maneuvers, legendary for their daring and finesse, showcased a mastery of the art of racing, often defying the limits of physics and challenging the very definition of driving skill. .

His victories were not mere triumphs but artistic expressions of his unmatched talent. Senna's driving style, characterized by a breathtaking blend of aggression and precision, made him a captivating spectacle for spectators. His races became events to be witnessed, experienced, and savored. He transcended the realm of mere driver to become an entertainer, captivating audiences with his unwavering determination and his relentless pursuit of excellence. His ability to connect with his audience, his passion for the sport, and his vulnerability during moments of intense pressure made him a captivating figure, transcending the boundaries of the racetrack.

Senna's legacy transcends the realm of sporting achievement. He became a symbol of national pride for Brazil, a nation that saw in him a reflection of their own indomitable spirit. He embodied the very essence of their culture, showcasing their resilience, their passion, and their relentless pursuit of excellence. His success resonated with the Brazilian people, and his image became synonymous with the nation's aspirations. His death in 1994, a tragic accident that sent shockwaves across the globe, turned him into a legend, forever etched in the collective memory of motorsport fans and the hearts of his countrymen.

Senna's character, however, remains equally important in understanding his legacy. He possessed an unwavering determination, a burning desire to win that fueled his every action. He demanded the very best from himself and his team, pushing the limits of performance and consistently striving for perfection. But his dedication was not solely focused on winning. He possessed a profound respect for his competitors, a fierce rivalry that often manifested in heated exchanges, yet always rooted in a deep admiration for their talent and dedication. He understood the essence of competition, embracing the challenge and respecting the opponent, creating a captivating dynamic on the track. .

Senna's character also revealed a depth of compassion and empathy that extended beyond the racetrack. His unwavering commitment to philanthropy, specifically his support for underprivileged children in Brazil, showcased a side often overlooked amidst his racing persona. His generosity and concern for others, his genuine desire to make a positive impact on the world, demonstrated a profound humanity, a side that endeared him to countless fans around the globe. .

His tragic passing was met with an outpouring of grief worldwide, a testament to his influence and the enduring legacy of his character. People mourned the loss of a champion, a friend, and a symbol of hope. His death triggered an outpouring of emotion, highlighting the profound connection he had forged with his fans. This emotional response was a powerful reminder that Senna's impact went far beyond the realm of sport. He had become a symbol of something greater, an embodiment of human potential and the pursuit of excellence. .

Senna's impact on the world of motorsports, his contribution to Brazilian national identity, and his unwavering commitment to philanthropy, all stemmed from the core of his character. His legacy is a testament to the power of passion, determination, and genuine compassion. He remains a powerful reminder that greatness is not merely defined by accomplishments but by the principles that guide those accomplishments. He stands as a timeless icon, his legacy a source of inspiration for generations to come.

Chapter 14: The Spirit of Senna

The enduring legacy of his spirit and determination

Ayrton Senna's legacy transcends the confines of the racetrack. His spirit, an indomitable force of determination, continues to inspire generations of athletes, racing enthusiasts, and individuals across the globe. It is a testament to his unwavering commitment, his fierce passion, and his unyielding pursuit of excellence, etched into the annals of motorsport history. His legacy, a tapestry woven with threads of courage, brilliance, and a profound love for the sport, resonates with enduring power, shaping the world of racing and influencing the lives of many. . .

Senna's spirit, a potent cocktail of ambition and humility, manifested in his unwavering commitment to the sport. He approached every race with an unparalleled intensity, a relentless pursuit of perfection that resonated with the very core of his being. This dedication transcended mere competition; it was a deeply personal expression of his artistic vision on the track. Each lap, each corner, was a canvas upon which Senna painted his passion, a masterpiece of precision and artistry. This fierce commitment, a beacon of dedication, continues to inspire countless individuals, reminding them that true success lies not in the pursuit of glory, but in the relentless pursuit of excellence.

Senna's determination, a burning ember that fuelled his unwavering pursuit, was a testament to his indomitable spirit. He faced adversity head-on, refusing to be daunted by setbacks. In the face of pressure, he thrived, transforming challenges into opportunities for growth. His determination, a defining trait of his character, wasn't merely a force of will but a profound conviction in his abilities. This unwavering belief, a cornerstone of his legacy, continues to empower individuals to overcome obstacles, to chase their dreams with unwavering passion, and to embrace challenges as stepping stones to success.

Beyond the roar of the engines and the thrill of victory, Senna's legacy is inextricably linked to his human spirit. He possessed a profound sense of empathy, a deep connection to his fellow drivers and fans that transcended the boundaries of competition. His compassion, a subtle undercurrent beneath the intensity, was a hallmark of his personality. This genuine connection, a poignant reflection of his character, resonates with fans, inspiring them to embrace empathy, to foster understanding, and to build bridges of connection beyond the boundaries of rivalry.

The enduring power of Senna's spirit and determination lies in its universal appeal. It transcends the limitations of nationality, background, or even the realm of motorsport. His legacy is a beacon of hope, a testament to the indomitable human spirit that refuses to be deterred. It serves as a reminder that through sheer will, unwavering passion, and a genuine love for what we do, we can overcome any obstacle, achieve seemingly impossible feats, and leave an indelible mark on the world.

Senna's legacy is not simply a collection of trophies or championship titles. It is an enduring testament to the transformative power of human spirit. It is a testament to the indomitable will that can overcome seemingly insurmountable challenges, to the unyielding passion that can illuminate even the darkest of paths, and to the profound empathy that can connect individuals across continents and cultures.

His legacy echoes beyond the racetrack, a beacon of inspiration for generations to come. It whispers the potent message of courage, determination, and the unwavering pursuit of excellence. It is a reminder that we all possess the potential to unlock our inner strength, to embrace our passion, and to leave a lasting legacy, much like the indomitable spirit of Ayrton Senna, the legend who continues to inspire. . .

Influence on generations of racers and fans

Ayrton Senna da Silva, a name etched in the annals of motorsport history, transcended the realm of mere driver to become a cultural icon. His legacy, forged in the crucible of Formula One competition, extends far beyond the checkered flag, resonating with generations of racers and fans alike. His influence, a potent cocktail of driving brilliance, unwavering determination, and undeniable charisma, left an indelible mark on the sport, inspiring aspiring racers and igniting a passion for the sport in countless fans.

Senna's impact on aspiring racers stemmed from his unparalleled driving prowess. His mastery of the car, a symphony of precision and audacity, was a testament to his relentless pursuit of perfection. Young drivers, witnessing his breathtaking maneuvers and unyielding focus, found in him a role model, a benchmark of excellence to strive for. His commitment to pushing the limits, his unwavering belief in his ability, resonated with the competitive spirit of aspiring racers, fueling their ambitions and inspiring them to push their own boundaries. They sought to emulate his bravery, his unwavering focus, his ability to extract the maximum from both the machine and themselves.

The legend of Senna wasn't merely about lap times and victories. It was about his sheer passion for the sport, his unwavering dedication to his craft. This unyielding commitment resonated with aspiring drivers, who saw in Senna not just a champion, but a man deeply in love with the art of racing. His passion was infectious, inspiring future generations to embrace the sport with a similar devotion. .

Beyond the racetrack, Senna's impact on aspiring racers manifested in a broader sense. His dedication to his craft, his tireless pursuit of improvement, served as a powerful message for young drivers. He taught them the importance of discipline, preparation, and unwavering self-belief - lessons that extended beyond the realm of motorsports and resonated in every aspect of life. His dedication to meticulous preparation, his relentless pursuit of the perfect line, became a guiding principle for aspiring racers, shaping their approach to the sport.

Senna's impact extended far beyond the sphere of aspiring racers, touching the hearts and minds of countless fans worldwide. His raw talent, his fierce competitiveness, and his unwavering spirit resonated deeply with audiences, transcending the boundaries of language and culture. He captivated the world with his breathtaking driving, his captivating personality, and his unwavering dedication to pushing boundaries. .

Fans, mesmerized by his brilliance on the track, found themselves drawn to his captivating personality. He exuded an aura of intensity and passion, a fierce competitor who pushed the limits of both man and machine. His unwavering dedication to his craft, his commitment to perfection, resonated with fans who saw in him a reflection of their own desires for excellence. He became a symbol of ambition, determination, and a relentless pursuit of victory, traits that resonated with fans seeking inspiration in their own lives.

Senna's influence on fans went beyond mere entertainment. His life and career, marked by tragedy and triumph, became a source of inspiration and motivation. His unwavering determination in the face of adversity, his ability to overcome setbacks and rise above challenges, provided a powerful message of resilience and the power of human spirit. This, coupled with his genuine warmth and humility, endeared him to fans who saw in him not just a driver, but a symbol of human potential.

His untimely passing, a tragic event that shocked the world, cemented his legacy as a legend. It added another layer of depth to his story, transforming him from a driver into a symbol of human fragility and the ephemeral nature of life. His story, a poignant reminder of the fragility of life and the importance of living each moment with passion, resonated with fans who found in his life a source of inspiration and reflection. .

The impact of Senna's legacy extended beyond the realm of motorsport, becoming a cultural phenomenon. His image graced billboards and magazines, his quotes were etched on t-shirts and mugs, his name became synonymous with excellence and determination. His passion for the sport, his relentless pursuit of perfection, his unwavering dedication, served as a source of inspiration for generations to come.

His influence continues to resonate today. Young drivers still aspire to emulate his driving style, his passion, his relentless pursuit of perfection. Fans still gather to celebrate his life and his legacy, to relive his greatest victories and to remember the man who became an icon. .

Senna's story transcends the racetrack, becoming a powerful testament to the impact of human spirit on the world. His influence, a potent mix of driving brilliance, unwavering determination, and undeniable charisma, continues to inspire generations of racers and fans, ensuring that his legend lives on, forever etched in the annals of motorsport history. His spirit, a beacon of passion and excellence, continues to ignite a fire in the hearts of all who embrace the world of racing.

Chapter 15: The Unforgettable

A fitting tribute to Ayrton Senna's extraordinary life and career

Ayrton Senna da Silva, a name synonymous with racing brilliance, speed, and unwavering determination, transcended the realm of mere motorsports to become a global icon. His life, cut tragically short at the pinnacle of his career, remains a testament to the power of human spirit and the enduring legacy of a champion. .

Senna's journey began not with a burning desire to race but with a deep love for the sport, nurtured by his father, Milton da Silva. It was in his father's karting track that he first felt the thrill of competition, his raw talent quickly becoming evident. He honed his skills on the tracks of Goiania, Brazil, leaving an indelible mark with his aggressive driving style and innate speed. .

The transition to Formula One was a natural progression, his undeniable talent attracting the attention of Toleman, a team that recognized the potential within the young driver. In 1984, he stepped onto the world's biggest stage, his driving style, characterized by a blend of aggression and precision, quickly turning heads. His daring maneuvers, particularly the rain-soaked Monaco Grand Prix of that year, cemented his place as a force to be reckoned with.

Senna's ascent to the top was meteoric. His move to Lotus in 1985 marked a period of remarkable growth, his podium finishes and pole positions consistently showcasing his exceptional skills. The Lotus years were filled with triumphs and near-misses, his battle with the legendary Alain Prost for the championship in 1986 leaving a lasting impression. .

The arrival of Senna at McLaren in 1988 was a pivotal moment in his career. Alongside Alain Prost, the team formed a formidable partnership, their rivalry becoming the stuff of legend. The 1988 season saw Senna dominate, his brilliance culminating in his first World Championship title.

His reign continued, securing championships in 1990 and 1991, showcasing his unwavering determination and relentless pursuit of perfection. The battles with Prost, the controversies, the clashes of egos, and the constant push for victory defined this period, solidifying Senna's position as a true champion. .

However, Senna's brilliance extended beyond the racetrack. He was a charismatic figure, his dedication to his craft and his unwavering passion resonating with fans across the globe. He embraced his celebrity, using his platform to advocate for social causes and inspire millions. .

Senna's legacy is not merely measured by his three World Championships, his countless victories, or his record-breaking pole positions. It is built upon his spirit, his unwavering commitment to excellence, and his ability to inspire awe and admiration. His driving was a symphony of precision and passion, his commitment to his craft unwavering. .

On May 1, 1994, the world watched in disbelief as a terrible accident at the San Marino Grand Prix claimed the life of the champion. His passing sent shockwaves through the world, silencing the roar of engines and leaving a gaping void in the hearts of millions. .

Ayrton Senna's life was a tapestry woven with the threads of talent, dedication, and unwavering passion. He was a driver who pushed the boundaries, a champion who inspired, and an icon whose legacy continues to resonate within the world of motorsport and beyond. His driving style, his passion, and his unwavering commitment to perfection will forever be etched in the memories of generations of fans. He remains an eternal symbol of excellence, reminding us that the true measure of a champion lies not just in the victories but in the relentless pursuit of greatness.

A testament to his lasting impact on the world of motorsport

Ayrton Senna's legacy transcends the racetrack, etching itself into the very fabric of motorsport, leaving an indelible mark on the sport's history, its culture, and its future. It is a legacy built not solely on his unparalleled driving talent, but also on the unwavering passion he brought to the sport, his relentless pursuit of perfection, and his unwavering commitment to pushing boundaries. His charisma, his daring, his sheer determination, all combined to make him a force of nature, a racing icon whose impact continues to resonate even decades after his untimely passing. .

Senna's legacy is evident in the profound changes he inspired in the world of Formula 1. His fierce rivalries with Alain Prost, particularly the iconic 1989 and 1990 seasons, pushed both drivers to the limits, culminating in races that became legendary for their intensity and drama. This rivalry, while often marked by controversy, ultimately elevated the sport to new heights, igniting fan passion and attracting new audiences. .

He challenged the established order, transforming the perception of the driver's role. He wasn't just a pilot, but a true artist of speed, a maestro of the machine. His driving style, a blend of precision and audacity, captivated audiences, inspiring a generation of aspiring racers. His aggressive overtaking maneuvers, his ability to extract the maximum from his car, and his unwavering commitment to victory became hallmarks of his driving persona. .

Senna's impact extends beyond the racing lines, into the very soul of the sport. He was a champion for safety, advocating for improvements to circuits and regulations. His tragic accident at Imola in 1994 served as a stark reminder of the inherent dangers of the sport, prompting a wave of safety enhancements that continue to safeguard drivers today. .

The influence of Senna's persona transcends mere statistics and accolades. He was a global icon, his fame reaching beyond the boundaries of motorsport, captivating hearts worldwide. His charisma, his outspokenness, and his undeniable talent resonated with fans from diverse backgrounds..

The Ayrton Senna Foundation, established in his memory, stands as a testament to his enduring legacy. It is a beacon of hope, dedicated to promoting education and social development, especially for underprivileged children in Brazil, his homeland..

Beyond the trophies and the victories, Senna's legacy rests on his ability to connect with people on a profound level. His passion for racing, his unwavering commitment to excellence, and his relentless pursuit of perfection resonated with audiences worldwide, making him a true global icon.

Senna's legacy transcends the physical realm. His spirit continues to inspire aspiring racers, his name is synonymous with speed and determination, and his commitment to safety continues to shape the sport he loved. He remains a timeless symbol of athleticism, a reminder of the profound impact one individual can have on the world, and a testament to the enduring power of passion and dedication. His impact on the world of motorsport is undeniable, a legacy that will continue to inspire and captivate generations to come.

Printed in Dunstable, United Kingdom